HOW TO EARN MONEY WITHOUT LEAVING THE HOUSE

by Daniel P. Richardson

www.meryko-p.com

All rights reserved. No part of this publication may be reproduced, distributed, or transmitted in any form or by any means, including photocopying, recording, or other electronic or mechanical methods, without the prior written permission of the publisher, except in the case of brief quotations embodied in critical reviews and certain other noncommercial uses permitted by copyright law. For permission requests, write to the publisher, addressed "Attention: Permissions Coordinator," at the address below.

Disclaimer and Terms of Use: Effort has been made to ensure that the information in this book is accurate and complete, however, the author and the publisher do not warrant the accuracy of the information, text and graphics contained within the book due to the rapidly changing nature of science, research, known and unknown facts and internet. The Author and the publisher do not hold any responsibility for errors, omissions or contrary interpretation of the subject matter herein. This book is presented solely for motivational and informational purposes only.

Info@meryko-p.com

Copyright © 2016 by Daniel P. Richardson

Table Of Content

Chapter 1. WORK AT HOME. HOW TO ORGANIZE IT 4

    Advantages and disadvantages..4

    How to organize work..9

Chapter 2. IDEAS FOR EARNING MONEY AT HOME 27

    IDEAS..28

    How to determine the price for your goods and services being a freelancer?..85

Chapter 1. WORK AT HOME. HOW TO ORGANIZE IT

Advantages and disadvantages

Today, it is not necessarily every day to go to the office, standing idle in traffic jams for hours to earn for "bread and butter". More and more employees of firms and freelancers are working remotely - plain fare (often even the kitchen table), without changing pajamas on a business suit. They communicate with the employer via the Internet or by phone, perform tasks, send them to the customer, take new and so are working day by day, making decisions on their own when to rest and when not to sleep at night, while working on a regular project.

Remote employment represents a working process carried out outside the traditional workplace and involving interaction with the employer by means of telecommunications and information technologies. Every year, the number of remote workers worldwide increase by about 20-30%. Leaders in this field are the United States, Canada, Finland, Denmark and Sweden. For example, in Finland, these workers make up about a third of the total working population. In general, the development of remote employment is a step towards greater flexibility in the labor market, which is the objective tendency for countries with economies in transition and in countries with developed market system. There are the following concepts that characterize the work out of the office: "remote work", "home work" ("work at home"), "freelance", "teleworking". Remote work is a form of employment relationship between the employee and the employer, characterized by the employee' performing of duties outside the office.

Teleworking is the form of the relationship between employer and employee if the office is located in other regions. Thus, home work and teleworking are the more restrictive terms than the definition of "remote work", that is, the components of remote work. The most common type is a distant work under the contract. It differs from office work only in that the worker is fulfilling his employment contract obligations not in the workplace but out of the office or at home. It is often the option "partial remote work" when an employee appears at the office only when there is a real need for this. Another type of remote work is above mentioned "freelance". Actually, the word "freelancer" means "free bearer", "free artist", "free mercenary", "employee out of staff". This term today is understood as a way of earning, in which the specialist performs a single or relatively few orders coming from different customers, while not signing contracts or agreements implying long-term employment relationship. "Freelance" is common in areas where it is sufficient simply to divide a large project into several parts and charge a small part to a specialist who is not present in the organization due to the small staff or lack of need for a regular solution of such problems.

Benefits for employees at remote nature of employment are obvious: the opportunity to organize the workflow on your own, a free schedule of work; there is no need to spend daily time and money to travel to the place of work and back. This employment is suitable for those categories of people for whom it is difficult to find traditional work: for the disabled, pensioners, mothers with many children. The disadvantage is the lack of collective (team), that is, the social environment.

The required qualities for those who want to work from home to become the only source of income, should be independence, discipline, dedication and professionalism. And in order to assess own strength and to know a lot of nuances, it is best to start the way in freelance with side job.

Telework allows you to be freer. You set goals and objectives yourself for yourself, there is no angry always dissatisfied with something manager over you, and colleagues schemers do not put a spoke in wheel. When all the work is already done for today you do not have to sit out the remaining hours - you receive the money for completed orders.

Teleworking also provides freedom in determining the value of the services rendered by you.

You are your own boss and compose your own schedule. You do not have to get up early, hurry, afraid of being late. There is no need to squeeze into crowded buses or subway cars, to stand for hours in traffic jams. Calculate how much a week do you spend time and money (gasoline, metro ticket) to get to work. Although it is not big money (however, in those whose work is far from home this can take a decent amount of money), but time is not small (on average about 10 hours a week).

Women do not need to spend hours in front of a mirror to do hair and makeup. Working from home does not require a dress code, it can be done in noniron t-shirt and slippers on bare feet.

Remote workers are not threatened with dismissal. The loss of one client is compensated soon by appearance of three or four others. If you are professional, well, or a person seeking to perfection and honing skills from customer to customer, you will not face a shortage of orders.

Work on a remote access allows you to spend more time with family and loved ones. And if you're a young mother, what could be better?

If you're a workaholic, you can work on weekends and public holidays, at least around the clock, there are no any obstacles.

A big plus and great opportunities work on distance gives to people living in the provinces, where there is unemployment and where there is no demand for such specialties as web designer or programmer.

At first glance, remote work has some advantages. However, telework has its disadvantages. If you are going to work from home, you need to have great willpower and self-organization. Not everyone is able to bring himself to work without external stimuli. For example, when there is no severe superior and bustle of the office, some people are too relaxed. They cannot properly organize their work process, since there are many distractions at home. In a person there is a feeling of total freedom when laziness wins a sense of responsibility. He would like to see a continuation of favorite series, drink tea with sweets, listen to music, read news in social networks, call friends. At the same time, really important things automatically are postponed. Working out of the office, there is no need to get up early in the morning, get dressed and leave the house. Therefore, some teleworkers all day are in their pajamas and have a sloppy appearance. In addition, not everybody is able to combine home and work responsibilities. After all, sometimes you have to be torn between a crying baby and a call from the boss. Another disadvantage of telework, as was already mentioned above, is the lack of live communication. Any person needs impressions for a full life experience. The daily trek to work gives you the opportunity to grow spiritually, to form the world view, make new friends and gain experience. With colleagues you can discuss office news and events spent together. When working remotely person drops out of society. Even if the company's staff member comes to the office, he will have nothing to talk with colleagues discussing the latest corporate party or last day of the birth of the chief. Therefore, working out of the office, you can become a loner who leaves home only to buy food.

When searching for jobs on remote conditions of employment a following number of conditions should be provided:

• Detailed knowledge and experience associated with the actions and practices of the work in Internet.

• To be able to carry out the work of the network and business relationships on the Internet.

• The high level of qualification in the chosen form of work in order to compete in the high labor supply market.

• With an average skill it is necessary to look for markets with low labor supply, or with the presence of a large number of vacancies.

• A good track record.

• The ability to self-positioning on the Internet.

How to organize work

Many of us do not even think how the efficiency can improve, if we stop turned into a home office bedroom, cozy, setting up on sleep sofa in the living room, or even worse, a dining table.

An important part in the organization of work at home is improvement of the workplace. Most importantly - make sure that you have it. The fact that you work at home, does not mean that you have to sit on the couch with a laptop or huddle around the kitchen table. Firstly, it is harmful to health. If you always sit in an uncomfortable position, or too close to the screen, you will certainly get problems with back or vision. And secondly, the presence of a desk and office chair helps to tune into a working mood. So try to identify a place in the apartment to create a work area in which there is no place for foreign objects. Keep on the table only what you need to work (computer, stationery, documents folder), and do not let family members to fill this space with their belongings.

If at the traditional work the questions of equipping the workplace predominantly lie on the head of the company or department, the organization of the workplace at home already at 100% is directly dependent on the worker. Therefore, it is in his best interests to equip his work area as efficiently as possible, so that it does not impede, but on the contrary, help to carry out the necessary work and increase its effectiveness. The organized workplace is an opportunity to have everything you need at your fingertips. It also helps to psychologically distinguish between life and work. Those who are constantly distracted by domestic problems, eventually complain of constant fatigue, a feeling that they are constantly in the working process, and as a result did not have time for anything and do not cope with their tasks.

First you need to decide how it is more convenient to work in any environment: for one it is more convenient to work in the maximum silence of close to other family members to make the work not boring. Most people prefer the first option, but it all depends on the individual: there are those for whom the second one will be more convenient.

Both in office and at home first of all order is important. Comfortable conditions actually is a matter of taste: one will be set up to a working mood by "mountain" of papers on the table, the other – lack of extra items on the table.

For beginners it will be easier to focus with soft music and the lack of other people. A little child can divert much, but for some working mothers it is inevitable. In this case, she must learn to observe the toddler and carry out the work.

Creation of a business environment at home will be contributed by the visible line between the work area and a seating area. It may be a screen of heavy fabric, rack separating desktop from the rest of the living room. You can also create zoning with light: set lamps on the desktop, suitable for office style, put on the shelf office supplies, folders, lockers, hang in front a business calendar or magnetic board, so you can keep a map of your actions before your eyes.

There are many variants of the original workspace arrangement. An excellent place for this purpose can be a loggia. It is possible to organize workspace at home even on a small winterized balcony, which can become your small office.

There are also less popular, but quite interesting options. For example, a window sill will be a wonderful workplace. You can choose to use corners or choose cardinal way to arrangment, such as the placement of the workplace in the cabinet or between two cabinets.

According to statistics, an office worker for a year spends about 150 hours on the search for lost documents. Interestingly, one of the twenty documents is not found. That is why it is very important to keep on hand all that you need for the work. It is advisable to carefully consider the location of the cabinets, racks and shelves for CDs, papers and stationery. In order to make the organization of the workplace at home was as effective as possible, it is necessary to purchase small drawers for storing all sorts of little things. At this, it should be understood that, cluttering your workspace, you will significantly worsen the conditions of work. Remember that it is not necessary to make the workplace a purely rational and practical. Do not forget about pleasant things, such as your favorite photos, paintings and flowers.

An excellent tool for the job can be a cork board, on which pieces of paper with a list of tasks are fixed. With this you can easily remove the stale marks and hang new ones.

Having decided to organize a home workplace, one should not ignore this useful thing.

Be sure to take care of your health. This is especially true for people whose working day passes at the computer or whose profession associated with a sedentary lifestyle. Do not skimp on a good chair, as low back pain and various diseases of the joints often accompany sedentary lifestyle.

You are sitting at your desk right in terms of ergonomics, if:

1. Your feet are comfortably placed on the floor. The surface of the foot should form an angle with caviar exactly 90°.

2. Knees should also form an obtuse angle with the body - it provides free blood circulation at a comfortable body position.

3. The armrests provide an obtuse angle between the forearm and hand.

4. The backrest of the chair allows you to recede to ensure the normal functioning of internal organs and muscle relaxation.

5. The seat should be sufficient, so you can use all its depth, and legs at the same time would not numb.

6. At the feet there should be a space that allows them to perk while sitting at the table as often as you want; allow yourself to arch the back, rocking on a chair and do the movements releasing excessive load on the body.

If you are using the workplace cramped space, then remember the main parameters:

• A minimum width of 600 mm countertops, preferably 760 mm (910 mm).

• Table height 740-760 mm.

• Behind there should be a place for at least 600, and preferably up to 900 mm.

• Height of hinged shelf above the table not less than 1300 mm.

In the process of design of compact and ergonomic workplace, use light constructions, bright colors and translucent elements. Secretaire is a great example of a well-designed furniture, designed for home office organization.

Do not forget that the place where you work should help you to tune into the business mood. You can visually separate the working space, painting the walls in a neutral color.

It is better if the colors are of warm tones - they have excitory influence and increase efficiency:

• It is believed that the brown color is favorable for a simple performance, and yellow and orange on the contrary enhance creativity and stimulate you to non-standard decisions.

• The use of red is recommended in the details - long exposure of this color usually causes excitement, turning into aggressiveness. But red tones accents will be a great solution, they wake activity and are recommended to bright extraordinary personalities.

• The pink color of the walls relaxes, and it is not recommended for use in the home office.

• White color is too neutral. It brings to the interior a feeling of purity, but it is very difficult to link with each other, there will always be something to look faded, and some - dirty gray.

If the home office is of small size, designers recommend to experiment with the cold colors, to expand the space:

• Dark blue - increases the activity of the brain, adjusts erudition.

• Green is able to "mute" sound, use it in the rooms when it is noisy outside the windows while you need concentration.

• Blue is a favorite around, it will expand the space and calm, and allow the focus.

• Purple and black colors are depressing ones, use them carefully, only in accessories.

The main disadvantage of the dark surfaces is in that dust content and traces of fingers are clearly visible on them.

Also it should be noted that psychologists proved that the pleasant aroma has beneficial effect on the efficiency of the working process. You can hang air freshener on the wall or use an aromatic flavor.

And of course do not forget about the accessories: pictures and images around the workplace should be aimed at the visualization of future and display your goals. Use the attributes of your field of activity, awards, diplomas and letters of thanks. Decor of workplace will inspire and motivate new achievements, keep your existing status and professionalism.

Arrange your work space away from the TV as the vivid pictures will distract you. In addition, it is necessary to make sure that the glares from windows, mirrors and windows are not reflected on your monitor.

The light should fall on the desktop from the left or from the top. An excellent choice would be light on the clothespin, which allows you to adjust the lighting. Proper lighting is dependent not only on the size of the room, but also on your type of business. If you work all day at the computer, then go to the question of lighting with the most responsible and serious approach - for you it should be important the choice of the light source, its location and brightness. If your job is mainly in making telephone calls, sending and receiving faxes, then it is necessary to approach to the issue of lighting from the point of view of its comfort for you. To work in a home office energy saving light bulbs fit, but it is better to choose the ones that shine with "white" light, not "yellow", especially if it is a desk lamp.

For lighting a home office, as well as for normal office lighting, you can use lighting systems consisting of diffuse and direct light. But in this case, preference should be given no fluorescent lights, and halogen lamps. These lamps carry a minimum load on the eyes and do not tire the human nervous system. In addition, these lamps save energy.

If the lighting system in your office at home is badly designed, in the average it will distract you from the job for 1% of your working time. This is 5 minutes in a day and about 2 hours per month! If we continue the calculation, we will come to a figure of 24 hours per year, which is 3 days, payment for which you just did not get due to improper lighting of your workspace. And that's not to mention the damage that you may cause to your vision.

It is recommended to use an ergonomic computer mouse, which is specially designed to reduce tension in the hands. According to recent studies, ergonomics helps to save, and in light of the increasing incidence of diseases associated with the tension of the hand using a computer mouse, ergonomic mouse is one of the most important investments in the organization of ergonomic office at home. If you are a designer, translator, writer, architect and most of the time working at home on the computer with a mouse, it is necessary to think about improving the conditions of your work and reducing the tension on one of your work tools - your own hands.

Also, the purchasing and use of ergonomic keyboard is a reasonable response to a large number of diseases caused by the position of the body and tension experienced by users of conventional keyboards. Ergonomic office keyboard saves you from having to bend hands unnaturally at work or raise your elbows. When using an ergonomic keyboard, shoulders are comfortably relaxed and your wrists do not experience tension or stretch; fingers, including the little finger, do not make unnecessary movements, moving from one position to another by pressing the keys. Ergonomic design lets wrists to rely on a suitable point, which reduces the load on the wrist area.

Thus, organization of a workplace at home is not always easy; the process must be handled seriously. The space, designed to make money, should be beautiful and comfortable. Organization of workplace home should take place in a good mood, so that eventually you like the fruits of your labor. In addition, a weekly "inspection" of documents and other papers would be a great way to keep order on your desktop.

The lack of fresh air and stuffiness can be bad for your health, which certainly does not benefit your work. In such circumstances, it is hard to tune in a working mood - you constantly feel tired and irritated. Try to enrich the space with oxygen often. You can use a fan or air conditioning.

Take care of the greening of the room. Home flowers also satiate your office with oxygen, which makes good impact on overall health. Also an important factor is the positive impact of the green color on the psyche. This is an excellent sedative, which also gives a positive attitude.

Keep the room clean. Regularly wipe the dust and do wet cleaning. Just a few minutes a day is enough to decompose things out and put things in order. But in the future you will not have to spend a lot of time searching for the right things.

Observe silence. Or rather try to work in silence. If you cannot afford it, put on your headphones or put sound insulation to ensure high productivity and that nothing could distract you from your work.

Organization of a home workplace is very responsible and difficult task. A well-designed ergonomic work area, established in accordance with the personal ideas, is able to give necessary charge of enthusiasm, courage and the inspiration to work.

It just seems that working from home you will free a lot of time, which previously was spent on travel, talk with colleagues and endless, often unnecessary meetings. In fact, when next to your work area there is conveniently located sofa and TV, from the kitchen it smells of cake and the children run around the flat, it can be not easy to concentrate.

As a result, often the entire day is spent on housework or empty vanity, and you have to work at night, when relatives went to sleep and TV programs ended. It is unlikely to sustain such a schedule for a long time without harm to health and performance, so you still you have to observe the regime.

Try to get up with the alarm clock every morning. No matter how great is the temptation to lain in bed until lunch, still force yourself to get to work right from the morning. However, working from home, you can afford a less strict timetable than in the office. When planning your day, do not forget to take into account your own biorhythms. It has long been known that people are divided into two main types – "larks' and "owls". The first are easy to get up in the morning, and the most productive work time for them is namely morning. The second, on the other hand, work better in the evening. You need to plan things that require maximum concentration and attention for the time when you work more efficiently. A routine job that you can do even being half asleep, can be postponed on the drowsy hours. Working at home it is much easier to be done, because there is no boss on your back, which requires that the report was drawn up no later than lunch.

Do not think that freelancers are entirely idlers whose main task is to somehow force themselves to work. It happens also vice versa: a person too keen on his work and not leave just for a minute of respite. Often, this is a "sin" of single people or workaholics, for whom favorite work is the main purpose in life. And if in the office twenty-four-hour sitting at the computer is unlikely, at home it is quite possible.

Maybe someone would think that there is nothing bad, but in fact the constant overwork can render you a disservice. It is not possible to sustain such intense rhythm for a long time, the person begins to suffer from overwork and cannot perform his duties well enough. The general emotional state affects the results of the work increasing the number of mistakes, resulting in broken deadlines and ultimately favorite occupation causes only anger and apathy. It is therefore useful to finish working day at a certain time, devoting weekends and evenings to rest and family matters. Try to accustom to it also your colleagues with whom you come in contact. Explain to them that the work at home does not mean that you are available for their phone calls 24 hours a day, 7 days a week. In the evenings and on weekends you can afford to turn off the phone and do not look into the e-mail.

We should also talk about time management - an important stage in the organization of distant work.

Telework is a real challenge, but it offers a lot of features and benefits to those who seek upward. The main advantage can be called a plan of own time.

Most people believe that the office employees work 8 hours a day. But in fact, the number of working hours is much less. The 8-hour day includes meetings, snacks, lunch, smoke breaks, conversations with colleagues and so on. If in the office an employee is working at least half a day, then he brings a lot to his company.

When it comes to working remotely, there are no restrictions in the schedule. You can make it as convenient as possible for yourself, for example, if your best working time is night, nothing prevents you from working at night. The main thing is to have good results. You choose the time.

Thus, to make planning of time easier, you need to identify the most productive hours during the day. In the productive hours it is necessary to deal with the most difficult tasks. When productivity falls, you can deal with solving domestic tasks, simple working tasks or phone calls.

After some time, the productivity restores, allowing you to get back to work, which requires maximum attention, patience and effort. With proper planning you will be able to provide the highest possible productivity.

Time management is not an easy task. For freelancers it is even more difficult: it is often necessary to work on several projects with different clients at the same time, in parallel negotiating with new potential clients. At this, the customer does not pay for the time but for the result. Whether you spend to decipher, to collect the content or correspondence two hours or a day - you decide. Therefore, self-organization for a freelancer is a key guarantee of effectiveness.

Proper organization of time and work process is the main difficulty for beginners in the world of freelancing. Those who successfully apply a positive experience of colleagues win.

Some knowledge comes only with time. For example, it should be remembered that:

- Specialization is important. If you are working in a particular niche (products for children, gardening, repair), then on the one hand, it is easier to always be "in the topic" and on the other – competition is less. Do not try to handle everything.

- Agreeing to work, do not be fooled by a small scale. Small projects require almost as many administrative and research work, and large ones.

So, we decided on the project and received an assignment from the client. At the same time, you do not want to limit your life only by the work: after all, there are family, friends, travel, hobbies. The lack of a rigid structure of the day and the thought that twenty-four hours a day belong to you, not to the employer, only complicates the situation. To focus on the important things, you can use the following methods:

1. Accurate planning of time which is devoted to work - for this you need to write down all your work tasks and projects, and then distribute in the diary in the whole volume of work. It is best to have a diary namely for such cases, then note in it what you have done and what was not done. Create a list of all the tasks facing today on the agenda, and then separate the tasks that must be carried out now from those that are waiting until the end of the working day or tomorrow, and so on. Tasks for which there is a "deadline" should have a higher priority than the tasks that you can perform at any time.

Keep in mind the importance of each task to avoid the situation when a secondary task forces you to postpone something really necessary for you. It sounds trite, but to do list helps not to forget important tasks, constantly reminding yourself what is the most important at the moment. It will help not to be wrong in setting priorities.

2. Identify the most fruitful period of time in which you are most productive. This will help you to understand in what period it is best for you to internalize operational information. Do not get involved in frequent tea drinking, as this will only deprive you of valuable time.

3. Apply a simple rule of "10 minutes". It is very simple: you have a work which you constantly put off, for example, writing an article; promise yourself that you will devote to it exactly 10 minutes, and if you get bored, you can postpone the work until later. Important in this rule is to begin.

4. Distribute all your work in order of importance: very urgent and just immediately; important but not urgent; not very important, but urgent; not too hot and not very important. Next to each degree of importance you can write due dates, full volume of work, and once you start to carry out work, in front of each task indicate that it has already fulfilled.

5. If you consciously undertook a large amount of work, and you are confident that you will do it in time, feel free to proceed with its implementation.

6. You can make adjustments in your schedule, but it is only when it is really necessary. You should keep everything under strict control, and every detail must be taken into account.

Properly budgeted time will help you keep up to do different things at once. Once fulfill scheduling, you will notice that it affects you positively.

Do not grudge the time to planning. Formulate a clear goal, but be flexible in its achievement. Prioritizing your tasks, you would seem to produce nothing. But the time spent on planning, cannot be taken as aimlessly lost. Planning in a global sense is not just priorities for today and tomorrow – it is the formation of a clear direction in which your business or your personal career will move in the next few years. Existence of clearly described (realistic) achievable goal, or at least understand the direction of development will allow to spend time and material resources more efficiently. Keep in mind that once formed a plan of actions is rarely observed "to the letter" from the beginning to the end. Leave in your strategy possibilities to respond to the surprises (unexpected events), starting with small changes in priorities and ending with diseases and natural disasters.

Do not postpone unpleasant things for "tomorrow". Sometimes the tasks falling on our way are not interesting for us. Most of the workers of intellectual labor will push this task almost at the last moment, which then will require hard work before job delivering (and well, if the deadline will not be missed). Much better is to do "unpleasant" things at once, or allocate for them certain (albeit small) intervals each day. So the tasks will be completed, and you will not have to force yourself "against the collar" at the last minute.

Do not try to be perfect. No one is perfect, so try to do a good job, but do not overdo in quality improvement. The time spent on rework of a good solution to the perfect one, most likely, will not be compensated for (if the idealization is not a separate item of the labor agreement).

To feel the satisfaction of life do not fill with the job 24 hours a day. No matter how brilliant employee you may be, you cannot hide behind the monitor from the physiological rhythms. Your daily schedule must necessarily content time "booked" for yourself and/or family; arrange a holiday when possible. Use this time to become more productive: rested brain is able to give faster and more sophisticated and beautiful solutions.

In the next chapter you will find many interesting options and recommendations for starting successful distance work in various fields.

Chapter 2. IDEAS FOR EARNING MONEY AT HOME

Some employees, having worked in the office for a certain period, realize that can fulfill their job responsibilities at home. They discuss with the leadership all the nuances and move to remote work. Other people deliberately seek employment outside the office. On the Internet, in magazines and newspapers, there are a lot of ads with a proposal to operate remotely. However, the choice should be approached very carefully, because many of them are fraud. The employer can offer round the clock to keep in touch and receive calls. Or, on the contrary, promised a percentage of sales, to ask to call strangers and persuade them to buy something. Even if this employment is charged, the salary is low, but the nerves are severely harassed. It is therefore necessary to study Internet resources, which present the remote job. There you can demonstrate examples of your work, participate in various competitions, and perform the test items to find potential customers. A great way of self-promotion will be your blog or site, reflecting the professional capabilities. It is important to show your own skills and interests. Particular attention should be paid to the forums, where freelancers write reviews about customers. Experiences of others will allow you to avoid trouble, because there are crooks among employers. For example, when the customer does not pay for the task and stops communicating with the performer.

IDEAS

INTERNET STORE

Online shop combines elements of direct marketing with the "image" of visit traditional stores. A distinctive feature of the online stores as compared with the usual form of trading is that online store can offer a significantly greater number of goods and services and provide consumers with a much larger amount of information they need to make purchasing decisions. In addition, due to the use of computer technology, you can personalize the approach to each client, based on the history of his previous visits to the store and made purchases.

The main problems of an online store are at the intersection of the Internet technology and traditional business. In a typical trade buyer accustomed to the fact that it is possible to evaluate the product visually, determine its quality and performance. In e-commerce he is deprived of this possibility. The most that he can hope for is an image of the goods and the listing of its characteristics. Often, this information is sufficient, but here the emotional and psychological factors come to action. Moreover, often there are problems with the delivery of goods, especially if their price is low.

Basic requirements of buyers for the organization of online stores can be summarized as follows:

- Friendly interface and easy navigation through the store;
- Convenient system of cross-references and other navigation elements, allowing getting the necessary information in optimal way;
- The minimum number of user actions (clicks, clickthrough, etc.) to complete the purchase.

The basis of purchase decision is storefront. It is designed to perform the following tasks:

- Providing an interface to a database of goods sold in the form of a catalog, price list;
- Work with a e-shopping cart;
- Buyers registration;
- Ordering with a choice of method of payment and delivery;
- Providing online help to the buyer;
- Collecting marketing information;
- Security of personal customer information.

Electronic storefront is located on a server on the Internet, and usually is a web-site with active content. The basis of the electronic storefront is a catalog with prices that can be structured in many different ways, such as by categories of goods, by manufacturers; it can contain full information about the characteristics of each product, and even its image. After the choice of the liked items, the user puts them in the "basket". At any time before the final registration of the order the customer can change the contents of the "basket" of goods and the amount of each goods.

Completeness of the information placed in the catalog, convenient structure, and quick search largely determine the success of the store, as here all the product information available to a potential customer is located, and it must fully compensate for the absence of samples and sales assistant. Availability of a large amount of information about the products on the site, in turn, requires that the store customers can easily and quickly find the required information either guided by directory structure, or by using the option of search.

A potential customer should be able at any time to get an answer to any question associated with the purchase. These are terms of after-sales service, advice on the specifics of payment schemes, and much more.

Owner of virtual shop has the opportunity to receive full information about the visitors to his website and build in accordance with it marketing system for online store. Software of online store allows you to not only gather for analysis the maximum of statistical information but to use it efficiently.

In general, the system of interaction with the customer with online store can be divided into five basic steps:

- Advertising, visits of seller's store by the buyer, browsing of the store, product selection, asking additional questions about the product;

- Ordering of the goods is carried out after the registration (authentication) of the buyer in the system and choice of goods;

- If the customer does not choose the delivery option of cash on delivery, based on an order made financial transaction takes place, during which by the means of credit card or payment system, buyer' solvency is verified, order confirmation of the fact of the purchase takes place, along with the write-off of money from the buyer's account;

- Receipt of goods takes place immediately after payment (information product or service), or after some time;

- The final step (if necessary) is a product support during the warranty period of its operation.

An important issue is the development or purchasing of software package for maintenance of the functioning of an online store. There are many possibilities of free creation of online stores on the web platforms based on predefined templates. It is also possible to rent online store in electronic trading platform on a dedicated server. In this case, most of the technical issues are undertaken by the owner of the trade platform.

COPYWRITING

Copyright is in demand, the amount of works is such that it is often "hot". And start an online business as a copywriter is easy. As proof of this we can again take the data of the aforementioned survey. 38% of companies would like to hire copywriters (writers, content creators, bloggers) with the skills of this work.

Originally a copywriter profession requires the ability to write commercial texts. This is its main difference from a journalist and writer. Commercial text should be created based on the knowledge of the target audience psychology, basics of marketing and advertising and PR. This text should be an active sales tool, it has to shape public opinion and values of the target audience in relation to the promoted product or service. Writing these texts implies the presence of the author's creativity, ability to find non-standard approach, and to be the "eternal" generator of new ideas.

Most copywriters are more satisfied with distant work than with the work in office. Working remotely, the man himself can choose the most suitable time for certain types of work. If a remote worker feels lack of communication with colleagues - he can communicate with them via the Internet, for example, using the authors' community. On such website copywriters can share their experience and knowledge to read and evaluate the articles of their colleagues, and simply talk on certain topics.

One reason for starting to write articles for the Internet, is that there is no need for any cash cost to start this business. But there are some hidden monthly cash expenses, which may increase if a copywriter does not care of them. Here are three of them.

1. Domain Name Registration.

Registering a domain name is fairly inexpensive. The cost depends on the type of domain. If you register multiple domain names, the cost will increase depending on the number of registrations. It is better for freelancers to create several web sites. Their number depends on the number of services they offer.

The more freelancer dipped into the sphere of online business, the quicker he will have to spend money on another expenditure:

2. Web Hosting and its tariffs.

Web hosting itself is not expensive. But you can also engage in internet marketing and that means creating a more certain number of Web sites that automatically increases the monthly fee for the use of different web hosting services.

Also you need to use secondary web hosting. As if all of the domain names will be registered on a single server, and it fails, then there is a risk of losing all profit.

In order to reduce the monthly web hosting fees to a minimum, you can organize the right amount of websites on a single account.

3. Diversification.

Among all types of online businesses, copywriting is perhaps the easiest and most inexpensive home based business. But, as with any business, you should always keep an eye on the bottom line - profit line.

As one of the features of such a profession problematic finding of a common language with the client can be distinguished. In principle, this situation is familiar to all the representatives of creative professions. Probably any practitioner copywriter has repeatedly faced with a situation where the customer for the hundredth time does not accept the written text and cannot clearly express what namely he is expecting from the text. To avoid such trouble, the client who needs the services of a copywriter should be able to competently prepare terms of reference (or "brief"), where all the tasks set for the copywriter will be accurately reflected.

WEB DESIGNER

Job of Web designer on the Internet is in great demand. More and more projects are developed precisely by the World Wide Web, and naturally require the creation of sites. An integral part of every Internet resource is the design, because namely the site's appearance catches the first seconds of viewing it.

The creator of the site design - is "an artist with a technical bias", or "programmer with an aesthetic flair". As a "techie", he keeps in mind a lot of requirements for the design of the site. As a "creator", he is looking for unconventional solutions to complex problems. In general, it is creative, friendly and resourceful person.

To create a site design, you must be both a designer and a programmer, and a specialist in the field of Internet marketing. The developer of site design has to solve several difficult problems. He must take into account the specificity of the site's content, limit of HTML standard, and also features imposed by the necessity of search engine promotion of the site. At the same time, the web designer has to manage to make the site unique and recognizable. Without original solutions he will not achieve success.

Web-designer is responsible for the way how the website looks and how it is perceived. He comes up with logos, banners and other graphic elements, thinks navigation, determines where to place the text. Designers need not only to create an interesting site, but also to consider its page load time. Creating interactive web-sites is a top class of web-design. To make such a website, web-designer should not only know the language of HTML and have an artistic flair, but also would have to know the "classic" programming and understand the databases.

In addition, web-designers develop banner ads, online greeting cards, electronic presentations. Many things you can do not having certain skills. If you are inclined to the creativity, it is worth a try! For example, to create a logo, avatar, picture or come up with a design for a business card, you can have a basic knowledge of working with editors and that's it. To create a banner, you can also use the online services. On the Internet there are sites where you can create your own banner in a matter of minutes. So why not take on such orders, earning good money?

In order to start working remotely designer does not need to learn all the intricacies of this profession. It is enough just to select a certain area, such as photo editing in Photoshop, and constantly improve your skills in it. Of course, the job search will be difficult, if you will deal only in one particular direction of web design, but at least you will be able to start somewhere. Gradually, as the appearance of experience, it will be possible to master new areas of design profession.

It is not rational to follow the path of many novice web designers and change ready layouts, passing them off as own. Firstly, it is at least unprofessional. With this approach, it is hardly possible to develop as a specialist. Secondly, if this will be noticed, a serious blow will be inflicted on the reputation. This ensures a negative review and termination of work with the customer. Therefore it is better prior to first orders to gain confidence, get hand on a simple layout and not to follow the path of plagiarism.

Here are the important qualities of a web designer:

• Developed aesthetic and artistic taste;

- A high level of development, distribution, volume, concentration and switching of attention;
- A high level of creative thinking;
- A high level of development of memory;
- Logical thinking;
- Analytical thinking;
- Creativity;
- Thoroughness, systematic work;
- Attentiveness;
- Patience;
- Orderly;
- Perseverance.

Major clients of web designer are:
- Advertising agencies;
- Studios of site creation;
- Individuals and firms.

Basic skills that are required in this job are the following:
- Professional skills of the work with programs Adobe Illustrator, Adobe Photoshop, CorelDraw, etc.);
- Knowledge of standard HTML;
- The concept of usability;
- Knowledge in the field of online marketing;
- The perfect sense of style.

Desirable skills are:

• Experience and knowledge in the field of creation and promotion of sites will be very useful;

• Arts education will allow learning new skills much faster.

In the basis of web design are all of the same basic principles as in the basis of other types of design: the principle of functionalism: "the functional means the beautiful"; the principle of constructivism, which is not in the purpose of composition draw up, but in the goal of its design creation.

In addition, the site thought in the technical sense, should be imbued with the idea, and only then it can claim to compete with other works of a similar direction.

You can search distant work of web designer on the forums of designers, IT and SEO-experts; in sections of vacancies on the sites of advertising agencies; browsing offers of individuals and organizations (all wishing to create their own website).

When looking for a designer working remotely, many beginners use the exchanges of freelancing. Even experienced designers sometimes are not averse to use the services of such exchanges, because sometimes very lucrative orders are placed there. To get started on these services, you will have to fill out your profile with an indication of skills and abilities, as well as examples of the executed works, if you have one.

Web designer also can work on his own site. Create a variety of graphic objects -. buttons, hats for websites, blocks, menus, banners, etc. These elements can be set for free access to visitors on your site. Surely there are many who want to download these items, especially if they are made with sufficiently high quality. Due to attraction of a large number of visitors you will be able to earn on your site, placing there affiliate links and advertising.

Job of Web designer is not only in great demand and highly paid, but also very interesting in terms of performance. What can be said is the designers are happy people, they are the creators, who are engaged in favorite business, getting very good money for this. The result of your own labor is always pleasing to the eye, especially if the work is really done qualitatively.

BLOGGING

Keeping blog or blogging is a profession and a calling, and a very profitable business, if you are lucky enough to become a popular blogger. Originally a blog meant personal diaries that people wound up on the Internet for friends, but now the concept of the blog greatly expanded – this is a site to the main content of which is regularly added entries, images or multimedia.

Popular blogs with attendance of 300-500 people a day have the opportunity to capitalize on contextual advertising, selling links, blog sponsorship by different companies.

Sometimes a blog is kept by the founder, but it happens - for blogging one or more authors are hired, who are paid money for blogging.

The authors of very popular blogs that are read by tens of thousands of people, can sell advertising directly to companies. For example, to do reviews of technics, Internet services, etc. on blogs. For this, companies can give them a variety of gadgets as a gift (barter payment) or pay money. The cost of the announcement depending on the popularity of the blog may be rather high.

Major customers for bloggers are:

• Private companies interested in conducting a corporate blog;

• Bloggers ready to hire writers to work for its keeping;

• You can make a blog by yourself, promote it and earn with the help of it.

Key skills required for the blogger can be summarized as follows:

• Perfect knowledge of the theme of the blog;

• The ability to find and tell interesting information;

• The ability to write interesting, so that people like to comment blog entries and forward it to friends and acquaintances.

Blogger' desirable skills are:

• Popular blogging "engines" of WordPress type;

• Markup Languages HTML, CSS.

The cost of the work of blogger is agreed. If the blog belongs to you, then all incomes will be going into your pocket.

Where the author of the blog (blogger) can look for work: on popular blogs, forums, of webmasters and optimizers, remote work services.

Author's blog is a mini-newspaper but its "staff" contains only one "employee". He is the author and proofreader, and editor. The reader seeing an article does not think about what arsenal of knowledge blogger needs to use to receive only one like. Grammar, style, HTML, SEO, design, and even psychology - a good blogger must be a bit of an expert in each of these areas.

In addition, bloggers need to properly dispose their time. By careful planning, it depends on whether the blog is regularly updated. In addition, in the case of a multi-authored blog, the author has to manage a team: the search and hiring of authors, content managers, the organization of working remotely and control over it. Blogger is a person who takes a lot of important management decisions every day.

The idea of creating own blog and at the same time the opportunity to earn money on it attracts a large number of people. Such an idea is feasible, but not all can implement it. Approximately 10% of people get to earn enough money on own blog, while the rest remain disappointed. Earnings on the blog requires not only an understanding of how to create one (it's at least), but also the commitment should be the highest. Understanding your subjects also plays a role.

Blog is advertising platform personality and author services. For example, if a person is hair stylist, he can start a blog about cutting and styling and leave his contact phone numbers in the upper left corner. An accountant can keep blog about changes in legislation and offer his services as a freelancer, etc. In the case of travel it can be consultation and compilation of individual routes.

Earning on the blog is reduced, as a rule, to the one thing - placing advertisements in various forms. Payment or for each user flow through advertising, or has a fixed price for placement on your site for a certain period. Also one of the types of earnings on the blog is posting links to other resources.

Making good money is possible only in one case - if your blog is popular and has good attendance. Regarding the placement of links - wishing to do so will find your whe a blog will start to turn into a serious resource. You can also promote your products and then have to do infobusiness.

Before you start creating your blog you need to carefully consider all things. Creating your first and simple blog is quite easy. Start with a theme of your blog, it must necessarily be of interest to you. This is very important, as it will be very difficult to write on topics uninteresting for you. The theme of the blog should obligatory motivate readers. It is not necessary to devote it to the most popular topics. Choose the theme that is the most interesting for you; there are a lot of variants: sport, flowers, children, cars, cinema, photography and so on. Ideal is to write a blog as an expert in any subject. Thus, you increase the number of readers of your blog as soon as possible. But remember that if you select a very narrow and specific topic – it will be more difficult to get a lot of readers.

When you create a blog note on uniqueness of design, choosing a theme (template), try to make it unique. Also due attention should be paid to the choice of the name (domain name). Not promising is to create a blog with the domain name myblog.com. This name does not reflect a theme of your site. It is a name that reflects the whole point of your blog, bears a significant share of future success, i.e. - attendance.

Following the publication of your first blog on the Internet, start attracting an audience with your friends. They certainly will visit your blog, and will comment on your article and leave positive feedback. Becoming the first and regular visitors, your friends will be able to direct to you their friends and thus increase attendance. Do not neglect a visit of blogs close to yours on the subject. Be active when you visit, leaving the interesting comments, and most importantly - do not forget to leave a link to your page.

SPORTS COACH AT HOME

Perhaps you want your own home based business has been associated with the sport? A good idea if you will exercise training at home young children. The essence of business is that children come to your home to achieve success in a particular sport. Many kids want to play sports, and would like to become the best among others. Parents unfortunately just do not have enough time on it, but your business will correct this situation and pass this problem on your shoulders. Sometimes a child needs additional instruction, it is necessary to help him to develop his self-esteem and become the best. First, you need to purchase the necessary equipment that would suit for different sports and with which you will be helping children; it can be basketballs, volleyball, football balls, tennis rackets, bats, gloves, and so on. Your task is to do business legally and that the state was aware of your affairs, you need additional insurance.

You will need to conduct master classes, to help children to understand the sports and tell them the secrets of mastery. Especially it will be useful to those children who have not been previously engaged in sports. It is possible to carry out both individual lessons and group.

It would be useful to conduct open lessons that parents can attend, so they see that you are a professional, and that the money they pay is not in vain, looking at how their child is developing.

This is a good profitable business, it will not only benefit you, but also help children to develop, and they in turn will always remember the person who helped them to become better.

Making uniquely designed products from beads

An interesting idea for a home business is the manufacture of products from beads at home.

Jewellery made of precious materials are very expensive. But other than products made from beautiful and rare minerals and metals - gold, platinum, diamond, ruby, emerald, etc. - there are fashion jewelry, made of ordinary materials or semi-precious minerals (crystals), which imitate precious stones and lose its value and relevance over time. Today, jewelry is in great demand among the women, especially popular are ornaments made of beads. For many people, the production of products from beads turned into a hobby. In addition to the pleasure of the manufacturing process for many craftsmen this activity became additional extra earnings. These products are fashionable and suitable to wear in all seasons and weather. Learning how to make products from beads is quite simple. To do this, you first need to come up with a pattern, type or shape of your product, and then stringing beads on a string to implement your plans into reality.

So exactly how you can learn to work with beads on your own? Internet will help you in this. On the Internet there are a lot of recommendations and lessons on working with beads. The main thing is to be patient and consistently follow all recommendations.

When working with beads you will need beads itself (all kinds of colors and shades) and silk thread. As the thread, you can use the fishing line or wire strips of leather. Also you will need elbow fasteners for attaching beads. In addition to glass, use clay and beads. This will allow you to experiment with your product in a wider range. You will be able to experiment more extensively with your projects.

INDOOR GARDEN

Flower business is of great interest in entrepreneurs who just choose a direction in which to work. Of course, in the first place, it is attractive for women. What could be better than to turn a favorite hobby into a major source of income? But do not forget that the business associated with the cultivation and sale of flowers, is considered one of the most difficult. It requires wide knowledge, extensive experience, specialized skills.

You can grow possible room and garden plants, ornamental flowers, which are used for bouquets. Cost of perennial proportionally depends on its age: the older it is, the higher its price. For example, the most common plants, cultivation of which does not require a lot of experience and investments are Monstera, Dracaena and Crassula (so-called "money tree"). The price depends on the species and the appearance of the flower. The only difficulty lies in the fact that the cultivation of such plants take several years. The main cost will be required for the purchase of pots, soil, fertilizer. Thus, even though, at first glance, the profitability of this business is very high, but the payback period is a few years, which significantly reduces its attractiveness.

If you do not have the knowledge and experience in the cultivation of flowers, seek professional help. Optionally, it is possible to hire an agronomist and horticulturist. It is enough if you have the opportunity to refer to them when you have questions about caring for plants.

Seedlings and other planting material of annual and perennial flowers are sold in the period from January-February to May. Experienced gardeners prefer to grow the seeds for seedlings on their own, aditionally purchasing new varieties each year in the sample. If new items "take root" and will be in demand among buyers, the next year they can be safely added to the range of products. Seeds are collected only from healthy plants, which meet all the basic requirements. In those cases, when it comes to early varieties of plants, seeds are collected from shrubs, fruits on which ripened before the others. Many entrepreneurs who grow seedlings for sale, are wary of hybrids. In addition, you will be able to offer your customers the opportunity to purchase a hybrid culture under the order.

At large volumes, it is needed to take care of the arrangement of storage space for seeds. It should be dark and cool. However, try not to take all the seeds "in reserve": the shelf life of flower crops seeds is much less than the vegetables. A risk that most of the seeds left over from last year, just do not rise, is too great.

One of the possible options could be the cultivation of orchids. Anyone who has ever seen live orchids, will never forget these wonderful flowers. They are loved around the world and are enjoying increasing popularity. Therefore it is possible to transform breeding orchids in a business without investment, which if performed correctly, eventually will bring a lot of money.

In addition, growing orchids at home is an opportunity for anyone who is interested in floriculture to turn their hobby into an interesting and promising home business.

Despite the fact that everybody likes orchids, not very many dare to grow them. Somehow, the majority believes that it is very difficult to grow such a beautiful flower in the home. In fact, the cultivation of orchids in the home is available to everyone. The easiest way to "fill the hand" is to begin mastering the art of growing orchids from breeding Phalaenopsis. They are not demanding, and learning how to plant these flowers you can safely move on to the cultivation of other more whimsical forms.

Do not be lazy, take high-quality photos. Throughout the season, place classified ads with flowers on the Internet at specialized and regional forums, bulletin boards, place advertisement in print media.

The hardest thing in the flower business is to guess the demand in the coming season. While some cultures have continued popularity from year to year (traditional petunia, aster, zinnia, chrysanthemum and so on), but there are plants that have become "fashionable" in this year. Foreseeing these trends is almost impossible if you do not read specialized periodicals devoted to gardening, do not go to exhibitions and to keep in touch with experienced landscape designers, who often create this fashion.

The minimum payback period of the business of growing flowers under favorable conditions is between 1-1.5 years.

MANICURE AT HOME

A good manicure - this is one of those little weaknesses, from which women are unable to refuse. Therefore, a good master will never be without work. If you can find mutual understanding with the client, she will use your services again and again.

Nail care services at home is a business without investment for women who know how to do not just a quality manicure. Many are able to perform it more creatively and professionally, than in any beauty salon. So it is time craftswomen to think about how to turn their hobby into a source of additional, and perhaps the main, income. But before implementing a business idea of manicure at home, you need to weigh the possibilities and abilities.

For those who are new to the provision of such services, it is important to objectively evaluate their skills. If you feel confident enough, and you do not have enough practice, it makes sense to take special courses. Such courses are usually short-term, provide the necessary knowledge for a few days, and are quite affordable.

If possible, try to work under the guidance of an experienced master. In just a few days of working with master, you will comprehend great smarts in the art of nail care than in a month of independent search for information on the Internet. You also need to master the basic techniques of nail build-up and buy equipment for the work.

All equipment - from nail sets to manicure and pedicure apparatus – should be professional. If you live in a small town and you did not find it, in the Internet shops there is now a huge range of such goods. Although it is not cheap, all the benefit of it is that at the initial stage, it is a real business without investment. After all, you can literally start with a minimal set of tools and inexpensive lacquer, and then gradually buy the rest.

Particular attention should be paid to the expansion of the customer base. It will take time and patience. New clients, first of all, will be attracted by your professional worth. Equally important are good communication skills and the ability to always be at work in a positive mood. Therefore, learn, practice, master new technology and be sure to follow the fashion, as it changes every year for a manicure, as well as for clothes. If you have become famous in your own circle, as a creative and talented master, you will have a plenty of visitors without any advertising.

Gradually this business without investing for women can be transformed into a full nail salon or beauty parlor. Especially if you cooperate with other professionals: beautician, massage therapist or hairdresser.

KNITTING ON A BY-ORDER BASIS

Crocheting on the order in the first place requires accuracy - if you cannot knit perfectly straight, you cannot see the good orders. This skill is achieved through patience and the correct selection of thread and needles. At first, you can ask for advice in a shop where you will buy yarn and needles, or look for an answer on the Internet.

It is possible to knit by order a huge number of products. It can e curtains, tablecloths and napkins, which is back in fashion and with fun are bought by owners of wooden houses and lovers of "country" style; collars and lace on the dress; and of course, clothes, from swimsuits and to coat. You can do everything, and you can select a narrow specialization and improve in it.

Learning to crochet can be completed for one day under the schemes in a book on knitting, or finding a special website on the Internet. Do not reinvent the wheel - just follow the instructions. If you do not learn just how to hold the hook correctly, then it will be difficult to re-learn, and incorrect technique reduces the knitting speed. But while knitting becomes perfectly flat, it requires a lot of practice.

Even if you have the simplest single-texture knitting machine, do not worry. In any case, it speeds up and can perform some patterns. If you have a modern multi-functional device with the software, you can make things of complicated patterns and styles.

Make an album of photographs of finished products. And stock up on magazines on knitting and create a folder on your computer with a selection of interesting models found in the Internet and folder with knitting samples and drawings that you can use in your knitting. In addition, get the habit to knit samples 10cm / 10cm of all the threads that fall into your hands, and make a catalog of them. In the future it will help you in the work, and customers will soon decide on the order.

Do not be afraid to combine. In one product, use crochet and knitting, fabrics and knitted fabric. Do not forget to embroidery and appliques, beads and lurex, metal and leather.

If you have firmly decided to knit by order, then you will have to allocate in the house a fixed place of work. There should be room for a knitting machine, a table for cutting, place for yarn, patterns, needles, hooks and other accessories. In addition, seats for yourself and the customer, and always good lighting.

PATCHWORK AT HOME

Another great work from home is a patchwork, sewing patchwork, or as it is often referred to - quilt. Those who practice sewing at home should pay attention to this kind of needlework, as the products made in this technique for many years not only did not go out of fashion, but increasingly are found in household items, as well as in urban fashionistas. At this, the big advantage of this technique is that it is not common, so the niche will only increase.

In what cases this technique is justified? It turns out that the spectrum of its potential is quite large. It is not only the famous quilts, pillows or traditional costumes, but also clothes, toys, souvenirs, women's jewelry, bags, backpacks, shoes, and huts for animals.

Currently learning patchwork in the public domain there are many books and videos. On the internet you can find specific lessons, download books and schemes of future products. So with this problem should not arise, you only need to have a wish.

For beginners, craftswomen the easiest way to express themselves are small works. If you are already engaged in the sewing by order, do a few things decorated with trimmed patches, add them to your portfolio and show to customers. It is desirable to have both things in the country style, and something super-modern, type of fabric and leather combination with the addition of metal and rhinestones.

Make souvenirs on order and for the realization, children's toys for the little ones. After all, what mother will not be enchanted by cubes flowered or patchwork elephant gentle colors for her baby? And constantly advertise your work, including at fairs and exhibitions. Only in this case you will eventually be able to sell your work expensively.

Breeding of aquarium fish

If in a childhood you were addicted to aquarium fish, and even more have an aquarium now, it is quite possible to turn a hobby into an interesting work at home. Of course, it requires some investment, but if you are not going to create a great production at once, then you will not have to spend a lot of money.

However, you will have to accept the fact that constantly under your supervision there will be many living beings, which cannot be left for long. But, if you are ready for it, then this business idea should be to your taste.

If you have not experience in breeding aquarium fish, you should start with the most simple. First, choose the most unpretentious for cultivation fish; this is viviparous species such as swordsmen, guppies and mollies. They tolerate errors in the management, willing to multiply and produce offspring almost every month (60 to 200 fry). Fry are also unpretentious and does not require any special care. You can sell them already in 2-3 months. Almost so unpretentious are many breeds of goldfish. Namely for this reason these fish are often sold at bird markets.

To work at home you will need: a large communal aquarium of 40 liters, two smaller ones, for growing young fish, for example 15-20 liters, and spawning, where the fry will hatch, for it the capacity to 3-4 liters is needed. You buy a dozen fish of one species. 4-5 the females should account for 1-2 male. It is better to buy adult fish, then you not have to wait long offspring. Find all the information about the kinds you have decided to breed and read about all the intricacies of management and feeding from the water temperature to choosing food.

Of course, you can limit yourself on the unpretentious fish, bring them to market on the weekends and have a stable income at home. But, if you want to achieve something more, then gain experience, you will have to move to a new level. To do this, you first need some large aquariums for a total of 1-2 tons of water, and secondly, if you want to make big money on small fishes, it is necessary to master the cultivation of exotic species, and those that are currently at the height of fashion.

You will not find such fish on the market, they should be looked for in professional breeders. By the way, you can start not with breeding and but rearing from fry.

Another tip: as soon as things went smoothly, just create a page on the Internet. This will be your online store. It should contain:

- Pictures of your fish
- Features of care for them
- Price
- Discounts, holiday promotions, etc.
- Offer related products (if desired, they can also be found on the Internet)
- Reviews of satisfied customers
- Algae for sale (growing algae, mollusks, fish feed can also be converted into earnings at home)
- Additional information (anything from anecdotes about the goldfish to articles on fish habitats in nature)

Over time, this site will become a constant source of new customers, but do not forget to replenish it with new information. The site on the Internet makes it possible to sell the goods directly, without middlemen. It is much more profitable than to give up your work to intermediaries or for the selling to pet stores.

Be very careful when purchasing food and the fish in various people. Substandard food or diseased fish, running into the aquarium, can destroy all its inhabitants. In this business there is little seasonality, the lowest demand for everything related to the aquarium - in the season of summer holidays. At other times, it is quite stable.

Of course, such a work at home will bring a lot of money only to someone who has mastered all the intricacies of breeding of aquarium fish. And if you rise above the level of traders from the bird market, this business idea eventually turn you into a successful entrepreneur with a solid customer base.

Home-baked manufacturing

The most important decoration of any celebration has always been delicious and flavorful pastries. Unusually decorated, stylized for certain event, it always admires the guests and introduces special atmospherics in any event. The greatest disadvantage of bakeries is that the production process is similar to the routine process. Of course, cakes and other products produced in the bakery are also aesthetic and beautiful, but with a taste of home they still cannot be compared.

Homemade pastries are always distinguished by extraordinary taste, special aroma, thanks deposited in it "soul particles". None confection baked in the factory will be able to circumvent homemade cakes for their taste. Baking cakes by order at home – it is a very real chance to earn.

Organizing a business of producing cakes by order is easy for every housewife. This type of activity does not need special equipment, expensive ingredients, and preparation time of one product is not very big. Production of cakes at home dynamically is gaining popularity among consumers. People less trust shops where all products are impregnated with preservative for long-storage products. Moreover, modern buyer wants to find an exclusive product and even with personal inscriptions.

The cost of a kilogram of finished products includes both products pricing and complexity of the decor. The more complex the decoration of confection is performed, the more expensive is the cost. Experienced housewives manage before the holidays to bake 20 cakes per day.

Making cakes is easy when there are standing orders. Naturally, the first customers will be relatives and friends. But, not to dwell on this, all your work can be placed in social networks, also you can place ad in the town newspaper and on websites. Some housewives do not have time to fulfill customer orders that come through word of mouth. Interest in cakes made at home is growing every day.

Accent the customer's attention on the fact that you work only with high-quality products and save on the products. Also very popular is the option when master gives the client a list of required products, and takes a fee for the work. Such a move is very risky, but it is also effective to attract customers.

It is also advisable to ask your customers, so they advise your production to their friends, and those, in turn, to their friends. As a result, you can achieve high-quality and fast advertising, without spending extra. At the initial stage of work it is better to choose easy-to-prepare recipes, but at the same time it is necessary to adhere to their attractiveness and palatability. With practice you will master a lot of different recipes, clientele will be accumulated, and complex masterpieces will be coped easily. The main thing is patience and willingness to work, then this activity will bring not only financial returns, but also the creative development.

In addition to the usual pastries you could sell pastries for customers with such diseases:

- Diabetes

- Lactose Intolerance

- Food allergies to the following products: walnuts, peanuts or chocolate

- Celiac disease (celiac disease in which a person has rejection of gluten, which is found in many varieties of flour).

You do not need to bake special products for shoppers with each disease. You can simply replace the problematic ingredients and bake some of the baked goods without nuts, or with less glucose. For diabetics, you can use sweeteners such as saccharin, stevia, and use flour with low gluten.

Sewing clothes for pets

All sorts of sewing business idea are better suited to creative people, housewives and mothers on maternity leave, as well as any and all people who are skilled at needlework and are looking to make extra money at home. Business for tailoring for dogs and cats allows realization of all your creativity and imagination, and while still earning a lot of money. Moreover, business related to the manufacture of clothing for pets, is quickly paid back and cost-effective.

Seeing a dog on the street in overalls or vest, probably every one of us will smile this sweet creature. Fashion on clothes for dogs begins firmly embedded in our everyday life. Increasingly, in the streets we see the picture when the "magnificent" owner walks with his glamorous pet. Why not take advantage of this fashion trend and does not take note of the development of this business idea for women? Especially since this kind of activity does not require large investments.

In order to start sewing clothes for dogs and cats you will need certain skills in sewing. However, it is fixable - you can just finish the courses. Very good, if you have a pet, then it will be easier to sew clothes and try it on a real model. And it is important to learn not just to handle a sewing machine, but ideally - to master the various techniques of cutting and sewing. After all, often clothing for small dogs is too petite, and loops, stitches, buttons, decor have to be processed (sewed) manually. You can gain experience stitching several different models of clothes for dogs of your relatives or friends, they will surely be happy to help, and in return will receive a cool little thing as a gift.

To open a business on the clothes for dogs you will need: sewing machine, material for clothing, the model for the demonstration of the finished product, a place for garments.

As a workspace a flat can serve, in which you select yourself room to work. It would be to design well your workplace, because it will also serve as a waiting room for customers.

Do not spare money, choose a multi-functional and high-quality sewing machine. Such a machine will help save time for processing joints, and its advanced features will help to decorate your product with finishing lines. If the initial funds is small, then pick up a decent version of used machines.

It is advisable to create several sketches and sew the first samples. They can be subsequently demonstrated to your clients. It will also be part of the marketing strategy, so you need to pre-purchase the first batch of material, without fear, and do not saving on these costs. Remains of fabrics can be made into a catalog, which will also be given to familiarize customers.

The main quality of fabric for clothing for pets should be its waterproof properties. In the summer you can use light fabrics, and for the winter - the fabric with warming. The colors and the quality of the fabric depend on the customer's wishes. Knitted clothing also becomes popular, so if you know how to knit, carefully consider the question of the manufacture of knitted models.

Patterns and designs of clothes for pets can be found on the internet or in specialized magazines and catalogs.

Several books can also be downloaded, with ready-made models and step by step directions.

The quality of work will depend on the cost of sewn products. But, if the model is exclusive, its price becomes much higher. The average per day one can produce 2-3 products.

How you will promote your small business its profitability will depend on. Advertising helps to attract the largest possible number of customers. The easiest way of promotion will be placing ad in local newspapers. In this ad, specify that you sew clothes by order taking into account all the individual characteristics of the pet. Ad on the Internet or creating your site can also help in promoting your business.

It is necessary to devise a system of discounts and bonuses to particular interest of your clients. You can sell finished products through the shops, previously agreed with the owner of a shop.

The successful promotion of the business will be contributed by qualities such as accuracy, patience, desire to develop and improve existing skills.

Clothing for dogs and other pets brings true masters a good profit. You only need to show imagination and offer customers a truly original and cute model. Consider different levels of dog breeders opportunities and offer not only expensive, but also clothes at reasonable prices. Use creative approach to work; you can make clothes with a focus on appearance or practical properties.

Finally, in order to receive maximum business income, you will need to offer customers additional accessories and items for pets. For example, the knitted clothes for dogs can be supplemented with a woolen hat, scarf and slipper. And for the summer models you can produce hats and bows.

VIRTUAL ASSISTANT

Quite popular profession is a virtual assistant profession, because there are quite a number of companies that need to perform a particular job and to hire someone officially simply is unprofitable. Among the tasks of these employees will be: to help customers configure anything, respond to emails; some employers offer virtual assistants to perform some functions of accountant. All the above work virtual assistant do at home, and besides this is a very competent step of leaders, because they do not need to hold perpetrators of such work, therefore, there are no headaches on the job in the office, social package and so on.

As the current practice shows, the tasks and responsibilities that remote worker can perform is a huge set. Creating and work with databases, travel, the publishing work, tasks associated with the medical theme. The functions that can be performed by virtual assistant can also vary depending on the skill of the performer.

Such work can be paid immediately after completing it; if the remote assistant task is a project, your payment will be hourly. A virtual assistant should be a phone, a computer with Internet access, and sometimes this includes the fax line. On execution of a task a certain time is given, the same applies to the payment - you can arrange in advance when and how it will be carried out. Wage can be a regular, as if you were an employee in the staff of the company.

TRANSLATOR

Translations are a convenient form of earnings on the Internet for those who at the proper level speaks several foreign languages. Like any work on the Internet at home, the translation of texts requires from the applicant not only professionalism, but also a number of other business, communication, and personal qualities.

In the work of translator, engaged in telework, a timetable should be obligatory present. After the initial familiarization with the received order and a preliminary determination of the indicative time of its execution, the order information is entered in the work schedule. Timely and efficient scheduling will ensure delivery of high quality order in due terms. In drawing up the work schedule, translator must not forget to provide for the weekend. At first it seems that, being at home, in a familiar and cozy atmosphere, in a conveniently organized according to the individual needs the working space, you can work seven days a week. However, after some time, no matter how comfortable are working conditions, fatigue accumulates. Fatigue rises gradually, manifesting itself first in decline in performance. Contractor of the order should not bring himself to a state of exhaustion. Much intellectual overload is accompanied by the emergence of symptoms of stress. Intellectual fatigue symptoms are confusion, inability to concentrate on solving the problem, the lack of perception of the information. In such cases, the need to rest from the communication and information sources. Fatigue occurs after a long (and sometimes short) physical or mental stress. Its potential danger is in blunting the will of man, his willingness to be led by his own weaknesses. In the person motivation weakens and a desire to postpone the execution of the work for a while arises. This attitude can lead to a breach of the terms of the order delivery and compromise the reputation of the translator. It is necessary to apply correct load distribution, timely good rest.

It should be noted that there are several options for remote work of translator. These variants are distinguished also by the customer type and volume of work performed. Two main groups of freelance translators can be identified. First can be called "non-staff translators", and the second – "freelance translators". Non-staff translators carry out orders for various translation agencies. Over time, they tie a strong relationship with several companies working with which is the most comfortable. The presence of several customers allows them not to worry about the stability of the flow of orders.

Freelance translator are working at a higher level with direct customers (factories, companies). In contrast to the "non-staff" translators, they are looking for orders independently and carry out not only translation part of the work. They are also fully bear the burden of the accounting reporting, workflow, and, in fact, a job search.

The level of payment of freelance translators, of course, is higher than that of non-staff translators. However, if we take the average level of income, it will be a little different, as a freelancer a lot of time spends on "non-translation", i.e. non-profit work while non-staff worker is quietly engaged only in translation.

Recently a phenomenon which is called a medical translator is gaining popularity. It often happens that in modern medicine or sports products are no annotations in some language. Purchase a good software for the translation of medical terms, place the information in all the places where your services can be requested and wait for calls. Also, you can help doctors explain about nutritional supplements and rules for taking certain medications. It turns out in a kind of online consultation. To the doctor was not distracted from the main flow of patients, he forwards calls to you. But this kind of home based business requires knowledge in the medical field.

Another version of a home business is translation of materials such as documents, audio, video, etc. If you speak several languages, you can easily find users of your services. You can not only earn good money, but also spend time with benefits, improving your language skills.

The main question that is of interest for the majority of novice translators - how to find a remote work as a translator. A good freelancer primarily uses "word of mouth" (i.e. recommendations from customers to their business partners and just friends). Also, freelancers often go to the trick and create an advertising site, which present them as a translation agency. Sometimes even the freelancer himself truly believes that if he created a website, he is now the company (although 99% of the work he continues to perform himself). For advertising, he uses a variety of classical marketing techniques.

The exchange scheme assumes competitive selection of specialists. Customers place here technical enquiry to perform the translation. Translators registered in the system submit their applications to perform the work, explaining why it is beneficial to entrust the order to them. The choice of the customer is affected by the rating of translator (which is formed by the accumulation of balls the amount for completed orders), reputation (the number of reviews from previous customers, the ratio of positive and negative opinions), portfolio (preferably to provide immediately examples of translations for the same subject), personal information.

For performers the registration on the exchanges of freelancing is usually free. However, for the use of the additional service facilities, purchase of PRO-Account or the promotion of their services on the main pages they need to pay. As with any kind of freelancer' activity, work at home on translating texts on exchange of freelancing requires guarantees of the order fulfillment. Therefore, it is important not to disrupt the deadlines and not to let the customer on the quality of the translation, as this may subsequently have a negative impact on the reputation of a freelancer.

One of the most important skills of any remote translator is the ability to organize his work independently. Remote work as a translator of English is not less profitable than working with some exotic language. As it was mentioned above, it is important to understand the difference between a non-staff translator and freelance translator. Starting a career best is a non-staff work for translation agencies. For a successful job search you need to know how to use search engines and have an ample reserve of patience. Specialized websites for freelance professionals have a database structure where your account is just one of thousands. Customers on these sites are not the most generous, and that is not unimportant, not the most versed in what they want to order. And it is also fraught with problems.

To write a well-selling offer to your account, you must remember that from the translator professionalism is expected. But more important for the client is to find a specialist for a specific project. Therefore, in the description of skills it is important to be honest, attractively and clearly define your capabilities. The main difficulty is usually caused by the last item. Customers who give work to outsourcing, as a rule, are busy people who have no time to read a long resume. Therefore, from the first sentence, try to catch the attention and inspire confidence, briefly stating your specification (subjects in which you are competent) and opportunities as a translator (translation, interpretation, simultaneous translation).

International certificates will help you to profitably sell translation services at home. This quality assurance is still trusted by the majority of customers. Therefore, in the first or second sentence it is better to specify your level of language on IELTS, TOEFL, CAE and other international system of language certification (if we are talking about English).

Membership in a specialized bureau is a special kind of work at home on the translation of texts. As an intermediary between the customer and the translator, bureau takes a certain percentage of commission. But here there are enough well-paid orders. The fact is that the translation agencies are included in the official international association, so their work must meet ISO standards and other regulatory requirements.

In addition, here they usually take really highly qualified professionals with rich experiences. Therefore, customers are willing to pay for quality.

REMOTE TUTORING AND COUNSELING ONLINE

Currently tutoring is not only a strong assimilation of knowledge and preparation for the examination test but an in-depth study of a particular subject. Tutor now is a professional in his area that can educate not only children, adolescents, but adults who want to learn, for example, a foreign language, and so on. Naturally, the work of a tutor is not only paid in hourly terms, but also it is depending on the level of knowledge and objectives set for him.

Due to the deterioration of the quality of free education, parents are forced to invest in the further education of their children. In other words, they have to use the services of tutors. And all would do if it were not a lot of time that is taken by the child's class, and which today's parents do not have.

Therefore, online education through private lessons and advice on an individual basis in the near future will become one of the most popular services. All what is required from the teacher-tutor, is the presence and knowledge of PC at the user level, access to the network and directly skills of Skype services use.

In fact, in order to develop own business in the field of online tutoring, it is not necessary to be a professor, a scientist or a school teacher. Earning a living is possible through the organization of courses for the teaching of information technologies for the tutors themselves.

Among other business ideas for one's own business in the field of online learning the creation of a special website with information about the tutor should be noted. Advertising services of tutors, you can earn a percentage of the orders executed through the site.

Another idea for business development in the field of online tutoring is the creation of a specialized resource - a platform for direct consultation.

As in any other sphere of services, business based on the remote tutoring is forced to compete. The most important advantage here may be the affordable cost of such services. It can be ensured in several ways: to reduce the fees for a tutor or to pay services of a programmer who writes a program simulator for different sciences - mathematics, chemistry, physics, language, and so on. Alternating the exercises with live teachers and the computer programs can reduce the total cost of the course.

The key to success in providing services to remote tutor, as well as in real life, is a well-organized workflow, sophisticated presentation of the material and developed training system. In online tutoring that should be given more attention. Lessons and materials must be taught at a professional level, on the questions asked should be given detailed answers in an understandable way. It should also be remembered that the boring and uninteresting classes will not give result. And this is a direct path to the loss of customers.

In order to start making money on tutoring, you need to take a few steps:

• Select the subject that you know perfectly and have the ability to teach. Most often there is the need for tutoring in the foreign language, mathematics, physics. These subjects are most in demand. Choosing more specific subjects, it will be more difficult to find students, especially in medium and small cities.

• Select the age category of students, which is easier to contact. It could be preschoolers, junior high school students, high school students, university students and adults. Each age group requires a special approach to tutoring.

• Select the most appropriate hours for tutoring, for students and for the tutor. It may be daytime or evening hours, vacation time, holidays or weekends.

• Clarify the price policy, taking into account the age of the students, teaching methods. There should be a system of discounts.

• Analyze your experience, skills and knowledge in tutoring. If you want to improve something, be sure to set aside time for self-education, obtaining certificates, diplomas, etc.

• It is advisable to draw up a plan to achieve results in the tutoring. It has to indicate clearly the time and desired achievements for the period.

There are several ways that can help to find a job of remote tutor:

Sign up in forums and blogs of tutors. Write e-mail messages on the subject, give advices. Having proved yourself an expert on the forum, gradually offer your services.

2) Add your CV to the sections of the work on the bulletin boards on the Internet, as well as remote work exchange. At the same time, for the bettersuccess, it is desirable to adhere to the following rules:

- Indicate the currently truthful and complete information about yourself (name, contacts);

- Add photo of good quality;

- Do not forget to express your attitude to the students and the subject matter;

- Describe your advantages over other specialists: teacher education, interesting teaching methods, etc.

3) Create a website or blog on tutoring. This can be done on a free hosting with ready-made templates. On it you will be able to objectively advertise your services. Write articles on the subjects taught, the methods of tutoring and share them on your website.

Being assigned as a tutor, you should have a very clear understanding of the objectives and tasks of training to achieve the necessary results. After all, namely the task determines the course of training, the intensity and scope of knowledge. For example, in order to "tighten" the careless high school student in physics, which he never really learned, you will have to start from the beginning and briefly go through the whole program. If you need to prepare for the entrance exams to the higher education institution, you will need to teach a few specific topics, maybe pass the exam questions. Properly posed problem is the half of success of training, the quality of which your payment will proportionally depend on.

LEGAL CONSULTATION ONLINE

Today, many young professionals who have a law degree, cannot find work in the profession. This can be attributed to high competition, because most employers are not willing to hire yesterday's students without work experience in the company in spite of the great desire and great ambitions. Therefore, many lawyers have to look for some other options for earning. One of such options is the internet work as a lawyer, as in the Internet you can find a lot of different options, among which you can choose the more appropriate.

One of the good ways to make money could be the work of a freelance lawyer or remote lawyer. Its essence is that a lawyer is working for a company and provides services for it mostly in proper registration of documents. Also, a lawyer can further advise on the tax, or the terms of employment contracts. Most of these specialists work for several companies at once. This is quite beneficial for both sides: for the company, since it is not necessary to hire an expensive permanent lawyer, and for freelance lawyer, because he can earn a lot more by having a few regular customers.

An excellent option of earning online as a lawyer is again to create your own website. On it you can not only provide legal advice, but also fill it with articles on relevant topics. It is very good if the young lawyer has enough knowledge to create a site. If not, then the development of high-quality site requires monetary investments. In addition, the money will be required on the website promotion.

In what ways of earning to stop depends on the level of knowledge and experience of the lawyer. More experienced experts can work on their own site, but the young need to gain experience in the writing of articles and online counseling. The main thing in this kind of work is to improve your knowledge and skills, not to lose a positive attitude and believe in own strength.

BUSINESS CONSULTING ONLINE

Business advice is also an option of remote work. These services are in demand, and professional specialists are always in demand.

In fact, business consulting is a view from the outside on the company. Sometimes business does not notice its own mistakes and stops growing. Due to business counseling, it can identify problems, improve organizational aspects, solve conflicts, improve financial situation, speed up the development of the business.

This profession requires a great deal of knowledge and its constant replenishment. It is necessary to:

- Understand the legislation on entrepreneurship, market economy, record-keeping;
- Be able to model and analyze business plans;
- Be familiar with the theory of limitations;
- Understand the marketing models, PR-strategies;
- Know the main stages of the competition;
- Be partly psychologist, to know the basics of sociology and business ethics.

This is not a complete list of the knowledge that is necessary to a professional business consultant.

Consultations may relate to very different aspects of the business: business start, business planning, company structure, personnel and corporate culture, customer service, PR and image of the company, sales. Business advice can be general in nature and analyze the company's operation, and can be highly directional and solve a specific task.

It is important to initially agree all working conditions. Perhaps, before your client has never used the services of a business expert, so he may have misconceptions about the work of the consultant or lack of them. Talk to him about the purpose of consultation, a decision of what problem must be found, on the timing of the work, how consulting will be carried out, in what form expert assessment will be provided, the value of your work, the form of payment.

The cost of counseling will depend on the number of hours you spend on consulting and scope of your work.

If intelligently approach to business, to organize your activities, conducting online communication, with the condition that you really are an expert in some field of business, you can make a good career and a lot of money. The advantages of freelancing, as well as opportunities for professional growth are huge - to develop personal and professional contacts with other experts and visitors, participate in contests, tests, real and virtual forums.

PSYCHOLOGICAL COUNSELING ONLINE

Counseling is perfect for remote work. Psychologists have become pioneers in counseling on Skype, along with tutors.

Format of remote psychological counseling is becoming quite popular and easy to use both for a client and a psychologist. Advantages of this format are obvious:

- Compliance with the border and security issues, both of client and therapist;

- There is no need to leave the comfort room and make a visit to a psychologist event of the day with the corresponding "arrangements";

- Since the safety is high enough, the client can have more trust to the professional and well discuss urgent topics;

- Presence of the ability to record consultations on voice recorder, for further analysis (for both client and therapist by mutual consent);

- The ability to get in touch and psychological support as quick as possible;

The equipment needed for remote consultation: installed Skype software, running (checked) headphones, microphone and webcam.

Remote work of psychologist has much in common with the work in the office. Admission is based on the same principles and methods, in general, everything is similar; the only difference is that the contact between the psychologist and the client is mediated. With online work almost all of the methods of work of psychologist can be applied, mediation does not hinder, but rather on the contrary, facilitates collaboration, for customer it is easier to open up and trust the professional.

Psychologists on the web tend to operate with a greater number of clients than their colleagues working exclusively in offices. This is due to the availability, efficiency of psychological online services and advanced audience composition. Skype promotes psychological services, it is a proven fact. Remote specialists are addressed even by such people who would not go to a real psychologist for one reason or another:

• People with an acute shortage of time: businessmen, parents of young children, etc.;

• Residents of large cities, where for the trip to a good psychologist sometimes one have to spend time in 2-3 times more than on the very session;

• Residents of small and remote settlements, where, firstly, the highly qualified psychological help is not available, and secondly, there is a risk of non-compliance with confidentiality;

• People limited in physical movements, for various reasons (for example, for health reasons).

Online counseling allows psychologist to use his time efficiently. All sessions are held at the appointed time, for the expert and the client it is easy to prepare and set mind, easy to switch from one client to the next.

Psychologist in the network receives daily a huge experience of cooperation in various situations, professionally improves and developes. Internet is an area of unlimited opportunities. An online psychologist has everything needed to achieve real pinnacle of success.

IMAGE BANK (PHOTO-BANK)

Image bank is a specialized Internet resource, acting as an intermediary between authors of photos or vector images and their buyers. All content is stored in the photo stocks in a systematic way that facilitates the potential buyers to find suitable images. Today it is the most common mechanism for the purchase and sale of photographic material on the Internet. Even staff photographers for news agencies, as well as artists and illustrators of design studios that have an employment relationship with a specific employer, often additionally use image banks for earnings.

Macrostocks are the photobanks working with professional photographers and high level illustrators. The history of many of them rooted in the days of film photography. Prices for images on these services can be up to several hundred dollars. But sales are not high on them, and for a novice freelance photographer it is unrealistic to get on makrostok. Therefore, speaking of photo stock, we will bear in mind the microstocks.

Microstock photobanks selling images on non-exclusive basis for the low price ($ 0.20 to $ 5 per photo) received a very widespread. The approach cultivated by them has proved to be beneficial not only to customers but also to the authors. It would seem - how one can normally earn by selling photos for next to nothing? However, non-exclusiveness of used type Royalty-Free Licenses when working with photo stock (RF, royalty free stock) allows you to sell the same picture dozens, hundreds and even thousands of times! Evidently, receiving regular payments for half a dollar from a few buyers is a far more attractive picture for the beginning freelancer, rather than wait for months that you will sell once exclusive photos for $100. Especially since the Royalty Free license allows an author to place for sale the same image on multiple photobanks. The amount of revenue is divided between the author and photo stock. As a rule, the author gets to 30-50% of sales. For billing virtual money are commonly used - credits or points (usually the equivalent of the US dollar) which after the accumulation of a certain amount the author can exchange for one of the e-currencies or withdraw on his bank card.

Most photostocks require new members pass a kind of "test" for the quality of uploaded photos. Poor composition or focus, noise, presence of artifacts can cause failure in the placement of the images in the photo bank. For motivation and expansion of customer network photostocks involve many different affiliate programs.

Shutterstock image bank is one of the world's largest microstock. The headquarters of the service is located in New York. Payments for photo and video materials are made in US dollars or in the currency of native country of the service customer. To receive payment for photos sold via Shutterstock photo bank, the author must have a bank card Visa or Mastercard.

INFO-BUSINESS

Each of us is an expert in some area of knowledge and outsider in some other. If you have a need for a good deal in an unfamiliar area of expertise, you will need certain information. It can be obtained in different ways: read a good book or watch a video course, attend seminars, conferences, trainings or go to a specialist for consultation. Namely on this infobusiness is built: one shares relevant information with others.

If you look at the process on a larger scale, the task f infobusinessman is to create an effective product that is needed for a large mass of people, and provide its best selling. For example, you write a book on the topic exciting many, organize an advertising campaign, set up sales (acceptance of payments, delivery of goods) and selling. This is done once, and the profit will come as long as your system is operational. And the most convenient way to organize the sale of your experience is the Internet, where the geographical area does not affect the sales curve. Internet is the perfect place for this area of work.

What infobusiness begins from? After weighing all the pros and cons, you decided that you are interested in infobusiness and want to join the "club of infobusinessmen". Then it is necessary to get acquainted with the classical formula, according to which most entrepreneurs earn money by selling their knowledge.

1. Choosing a niche, such as personal growth, health, relationships, Web design, etc. From this step depends on how much money you will receive in the end, as each of the areas has its own potential, the level of demand.

2. Create a website or blog on a suitable subject, it is the main stage. For example, you have chosen a niche "Health", then the site might be, for example, about the treatment of diseases in the home.

3. Filling the site with useful content: articles, videos or audio recordings.

4. Attracting audience to your site. For this purpose, a variety of advertising methods are used, and the site is optimized.

5. Create a mailing list. With each letter the reader has more confidence in you, at least to this you should strive. Trust of the people is the key to success.

6. At the same time, make your information products (book, video tutorials, software, and so on). As a rule, it is free. Work on the second product (paid) and by slow steps lead your readers to its release – create their interest.

7. Tell your audience about the release of new product, earn money on its sale.

This short chain is only the beginning of earnings. There are other formulas that allow departing from the above system, but the essence is the same. There are ways in which you do not need to create a product, but rather to promote other people's, for example, a way to earn money online as affiliate program will help you in this. The site itself brings the owner a profit, becoming a place to advertise and promote other people's information products.

Goods in infobusiness is "packed" and "useful" information. For example, infobusiness products are e-books (in pdf format or mp3 format) all kinds of audio, video, webinars, audio and video training, articles (copywriting or rewriting), photobanks, sites, accompanying web services, etc.

Among all types of earnings in the Internet, this business can be attributed to the category of the most lucrative and profitable. Let us look at the benefits of this type of activity:

- Very low cost of creating info-products (provided that you are very well versed in any subject, but if you are not a pro in something, you can always find someone who knows more and better than you);

- Your information products are sold on the web 24 hours a day, 7 days a week. By doing the work once and automate the whole process, you can make a profit away from your computer;

- Instant delivery of info-product to customers (if the item is on removable media, the delivery process can be delegated and you will enjoy your free time);

- All profits from sales remains with you 100% (if you carry out the sale yourself);

- Created a product once, you can sell an infinite number of copies (from time to time you will have to update it so that it was urgent to date);

- A huge target audience;

- Relatively low cost of info-products.

How to determine the price for your goods and services being a freelancer?

For all beginners in freelancing, this question is one of the major before starting work. What price should I set for my services? It is clear that everyone wants to earn more (why should we dissemble?). But at the same time any sane person understands that for no reason nobody will pay big money to unknown freelancer.

However, do not put too low price. Yes, it is clear that in any case the beginner has to first take up the most menial and "black" work. But it is the wrong view that the low prices will provide a huge influx of customers. Even if this suddenly happens, then the profit will be still negligible, and you simply will not be able to cope with the volume of work. As a result, customers will simply leave you to the place where, perhaps, they would pay more, but never have problems with the timing and quality.

You can afford reducing the price only in one case (but this, again, only very experienced freelancers can do) - when you in some way optimized the work process and execute it in two to three times faster than competitors.

In simpler terms, the drop in prices or a permanent work at low prices is a road to nowhere.

What can be recommended not only for beginners but also experienced freelancer? Exclusivity - get in your work and skills something that others do not have, and in detail (argumentatively) tell about it. And if you manage to become a "monopolist" in any field, so it is just great! PR – good resume and portfolio with a selection of your best work – not one time will help your business.

Be able to reasonably justify your prices by listing and explaining what the client will receive by buying your work. It has long been no secret that the profit of customers is at times more than the amount that they pay freelancers. Text, graphics, and so on - all this makes a profit, and not a single but regular.

Work efficiently. Yes, it sounds corny, but, unfortunately, this is the problem with many freelancers. Positioning yourself not only with words, but also deeds, as a reliable and accurate performer, you can more quickly gain popularity among customers. Hence it follows also the level of service - always be polite with people, respond to emails as soon as possible, deliver the work in good design. This "wrapping" would be appreciated by many.

Engage in self-development. This is an investment in your future. Improve your skills, learn new things, participate in discussion forums. It is possible that for any information you have to pay (courses, seminars, webinars), and perhaps you should not be stingy, because it all comes back to you in the form of well-paid orders, respect in the professional environment and demand from customers.

www.ingramcontent.com/pod-product-compliance
Lightning Source LLC
Chambersburg PA
CBHW070109210526
45170CB00013B/797